Maddy Moona's Menagerie

"Coloured Bedtime StoryBook"

By

Rachel Zadok

Illustrated by

Candace di Talamo

ILLUSTRATED & PUBLISHED
BY
E-KİTAP PROJESİ & CHEAPEST BOOKS

www.cheapestboooks.com

 www.facebook.com/EKitapProjesi

ISBN: 978-625-6308-64-0

Copyright, 2024 by e-Kitap Projesi
Istanbul

Categories: Adventure, Community
Country of Origin: United States
Cover: © Cheapest Books
License: CC-BY-4.0

For full terms of use and attribution, http://creativecommons.org/licenses/by/4.0/

Narrator: Sharp

© **All rights reserved**.

Except for the conditions stated in the License, no part of this book shall be reproduced or transmitted in any form or by any means, electronic or mechanical, including photocopy, recording or by any information or retrieval system, without written permission form the publisher.

About the Book

It's Maddy Moona's birthday and she really wants a pet!

But which silly animal will picky Maddy get?

My name is Maddy Moona, and today I'm turning five. Dad promised I could choose a pet, a real one! Something live! We'll travel across the whole wide world, searching Mali through Tibet, until we find the perfect one... Oh, I know just what I'll get!

I'm going to get an elephant. I'll ride on it to school. My brother Billy can walk behind, he'll think I'm awfully cool. But... what if Ellie caught a cold? I guess she'd sneeze.... A LOT! There is no tissue big enough to wipe up all that snot.

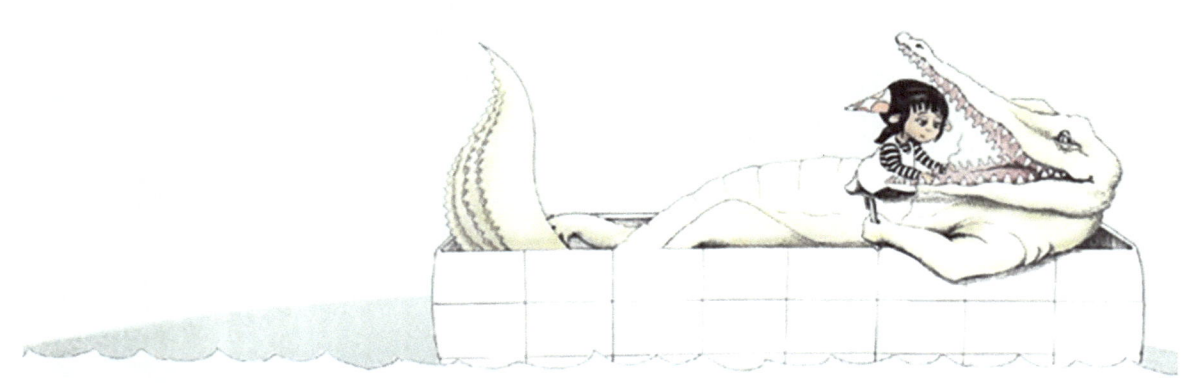

I want a Nile crocodile sent to me by the pharaohs. I'll call him Tut and feed him soup, fish fingers, and baby marrows. I'll keep him in the bathtub and brush his pearly whites. But... what if flossing all those teeth takes me all day and night?

Perhaps a pair of porcupines, for games of robbers and cops. Their prickly quills will be handy for holding up sweetie shops. I can munch away on candy bars while my gang sharpen their spines. But... what if my sharp-shooting pals put me in the firing line?

Maybe I need a stealthier plan. Let's clear out the store with funk! There isn't a smellier critter on earth. That's what I want – a skunk! But... what if I can't go into the shop after Skunky has let off his stink? Sweets are no good for my teeth anyway. A rotten idea! I need to rethink!

A rhino! The horns, the big stomping feet, the armour on both of its flanks! Billy would never chase me again. It would be my own personal tank. But... what if Billy raises his temper and Rhino goes on the rampage? Crash bang boom! The teacups! The plates! Now I'm grounded 'til I'm gran's age.

I need a beast to tame my brother. With teeth, sharp claws and a roar. A LION! I could feed it Billy biltong... Yes! A lion would settle the score. But... a lion has a huge appetite. Skinny Billy won't satisfy. And once Brutus has a taste for us Moonas, he'll see me as Maddy stir-fry.

Dad thinks I should choose a cuddlier pet. My parents are so hard to please. They want me to have a pet I can hug. A python? A python has squeeze. But... if Snakey develops too much of a crush, he'll suffocate me with affection. To be honest, I just can't marry a snake! And reptiles can't handle rejection.

No, reptiles aren't the way to go. I definitely need something taller. A giraffe would be awesome. I'll slide down her neck, and think up a long name to call her. But... something more than eight foot tall is no good. Our house has a rather low ceiling. I'd spend hours massaging cricks out her neck. My fingers would lose all their feeling.

None of these are the perfect pet! Oh what, oh what will I get?

Those animals just don't work. None are my perfect partner in crime. I want something with fur, a pet who will follow. Oh wait! I know – a canine!

My Bandit is the biggest bark on the block! He's the fastest pup in the west! Nothing can stop us. Not Billy nor bedtime. I love my Bandit. He's my best!

End of the Story

www.ingramcontent.com/pod-product-compliance
Lightning Source LLC
LaVergne TN
LVHW070454080526
838202LV00035B/2835